Lucy's Baby Brother

by Althea Hayton

drawings by John Farrell

front cover design by Amber Wilson, aged 4 years

Eddington Press, St. Albans, 1995

Lucy's Mum was getting very fat. That was because there was a baby growing inside her. Every day Lucy put her face against her Mummy's tummy and she could feel the new baby wiggling and squiggling about.

Then one day, it was Monday, and time for the baby to be born. Lucy stayed with Grandma while Daddy drove Mummy to the hospital. Lucy wished she could be with Mummy too. She was very excited.

On Tuesday morning, Lucy woke up and Daddy was there. "Has the baby come out?" asked Lucy.

Daddy said. "Yes the baby has come out, and we have called him Tom. I'm afraid you can't go and see him today, because he is very poorly."

Lucy made a lovely picture to give to Baby Tom when he was better.

On Wednesday, Daddy said, "Baby Tom got so poorly in the night that he has died." Daddy had a big tear on his cheek because he was so sad. Lucy gave Daddy a big hug to make it better.

"Can I see baby Tom?" asked Lucy. Daddy and Grandma looked at each other. Then Daddy said: "Let's go and see Mummy and I'll show you baby Tom too."

"Can I take my picture?" asked Lucy.
"Of course you can," said Daddy.

In the car Lucy asked: "Can I hold baby Tom?" "Yes," said Daddy. "Will he be crying?" asked Lucy. "No," said Daddy. "He will be very still and quiet."

When they got to the hospital, Daddy and Lucy went to Mummy's room. Lucy sat on Mummy's bed and gave her a big kiss. Mummy didn't say anything because she was very, very sad.

Lucy got off the bed. “Can I give Tom his picture now?”

Mummy said, “Yes, you can. He’s over there.”

Daddy fetched the basket and there was baby Tom lying in it wrapped in a white shawl. Mummy took him out and cuddled him for a while. There was a big tear on her cheek. Lucy showed the baby the picture but he couldn’t look at it because his eyes were closed.

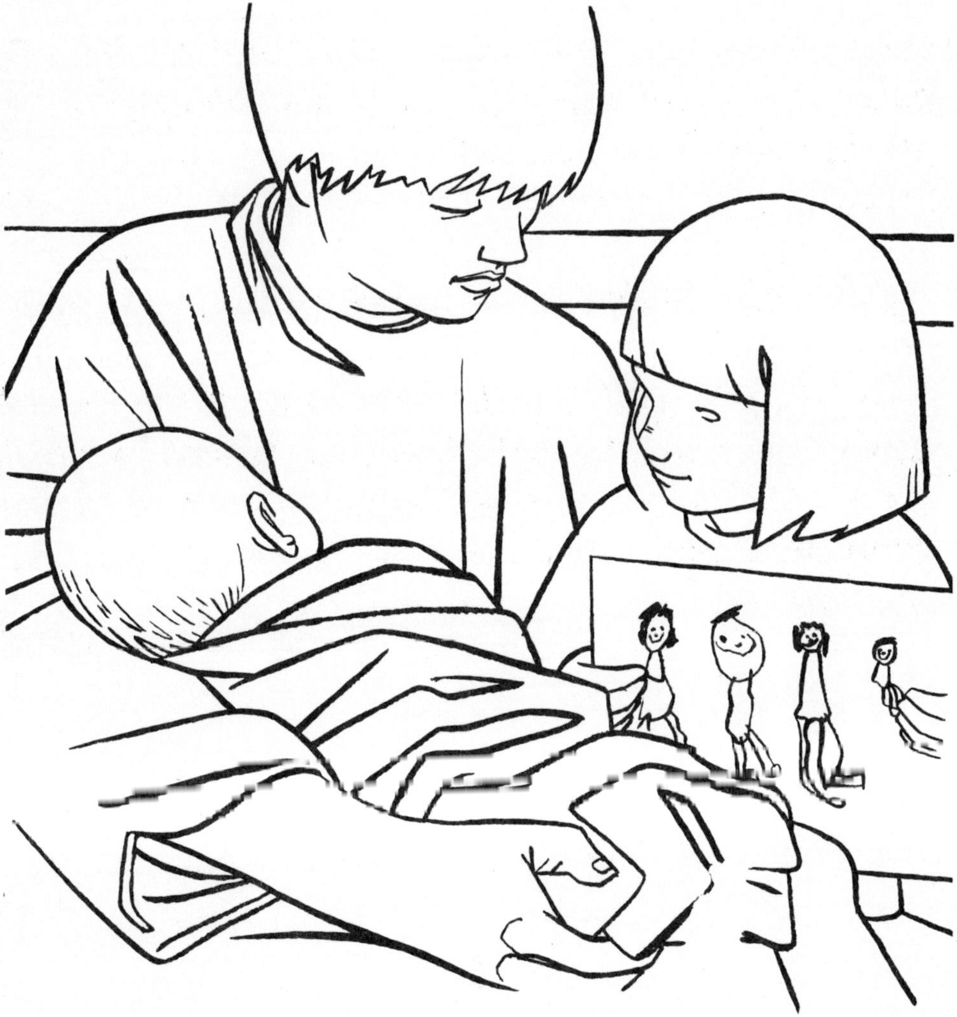

"Can I hold him?" asked Lucy. Daddy sat her down in the big armchair, and laid baby Tom on her lap. He was very still and quiet and did not move.

"He has died, hasn't he?" asked Lucy.

"Yes, Lucy," said Daddy. "He was so poorly he couldn't live any more. But we can cuddle him and talk to him as much as we like until it is time to say goodbye to him."

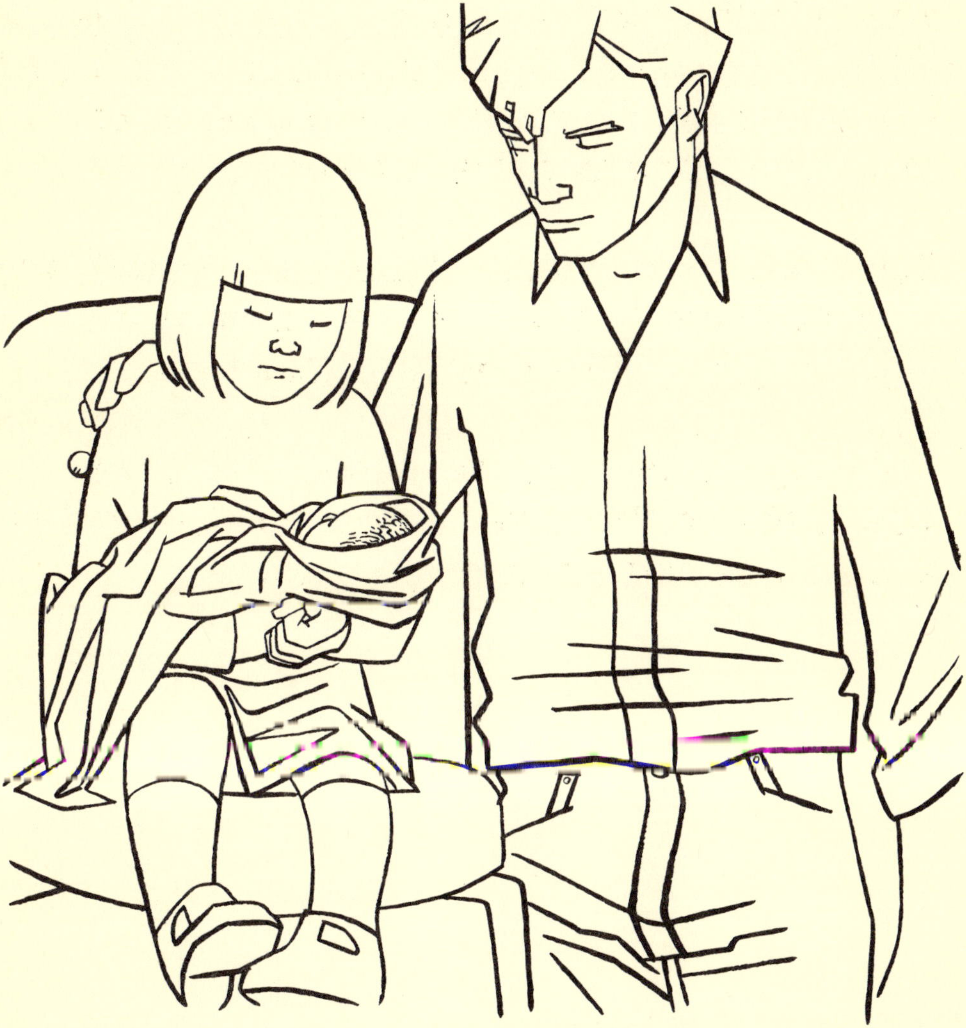

On Thursday Lucy went to see Mummy again, to fetch her home from the hospital. Baby Tom would not be coming home because he had to stay in the special place for babies who had died.

They took some photos of Lucy and Daddy and Mummy holding baby Tom, and some of him on his own - even one without any clothes on!

Lucy touched him with her hand and felt him. He was quite cold. Then they all said goodbye to Tom and the nice nurse who took him away.

Back home, they all went into baby Tom's room, where the cot and the teddy were waiting for him. Everyone was very sad because he couldn't come home.

Lucy put her picture in the cot because baby Tom wasn't there. She whispered to herself: "I love you, Baby Tom."

The next Monday they all made a funeral for baby Tom at the cemetery. Everyone had a flower to carry. Lucy held her flower very carefully. It was her second present for baby Tom.

The man had made a hole in the ground and Daddy put a little wooden box into the hole. Mummy said that baby Tom was inside, but Lucy couldn't see him.

The priest was there and he said a special prayer for baby Tom. Afterwards everyone put a flower by the grave to say: "We love you, Baby Tom." Lucy put her flower with Mummy's and Daddy's.

Mummy and Daddy put baby Tom's things away in a box and put it in the cupboard. Mummy told Lucy that one day there might be another baby to sleep in Tom's room.

They put Lucy's picture on the wall in her room with the photograph of Lucy and Tom. Lucy could see it every night when she went to bed.

At school Lucy told her teacher that her baby had died. She showed everyone her picture.

Teacher let Lucy tell the other children her story about the hospital and the flowers and the hole in the ground. It made Lucy cry a little bit but she wanted to say it.

Her teacher gave Lucy a special cuddle because she was sad and it made her tummy hurt. Lucy was crying because baby Tom couldn't ever come home to live with them.

Lucy is six now, and has a new baby brother called Sam. It is baby Tom's birthday today, and Lucy and Sam are going with Mummy and Daddy to the special place in the cemetery. Lucy has a flower for baby Tom. She can read the words on the grave. They say: "Baby Tom."

Lucy can't see her baby brother any more, but she can talk to him. Lucy whispers very softly: "We only saw you for a little while, Baby Tom, but we will love you for ever."

BABY
TOM
born
26.9.94
died
27.9.94

For further help, support and information -

Alder Centre
Royal Liverpool Children's NHS Trust
Alder Hey, Eaton Road, Liverpool L12 2AP
Helpline Tel: 0151 228 9759 (evenings)
Counselling and support for anyone who is affected by the death of a child.

SANDS (The Stillbirth and Neonatal Death Society)
28 Portland Place, London W1N 4DE
Helpline Tel: 0171 436 5881
Information, local support groups for bereaved parents

Blisslink Nippers
17-21 Emerald Street, London WC1N 3QL
Tel: 0171 831 9393/8996
Parent support and information service for babies on life support.
"Special memories" bereavement group.

Compassionate Friends
53 North Street, Bristol BS3 1EW
Tel: 0117 953 9639
An internationall organisation of bereaved parents offering friendship and understanding to other bereaved parents.

Child Bereavement Trust
1 Millside, Riversdale, Bourne End, Bucks. SL8 5EB
Tel: 01494 765001
Support and counselling for grieving families, training and support for professionals.

CRUSE
Cruse House, 126 Sheen Road, Richmond, Surrey TW9 1UR
Tel: 0181 940 4818
Counsellors, support for bereaved, training and literature about bereavement.

Multiple Births Foundation
Queen Charlotte's and Chelsea Hospital
Goldhawk Road, London W6 0XG
Tel: 0181 740 3519
For families of twins and higher-older births. Has a bereavement clinic.

"Remember our Child"
50 University Street, Belfast BT7 1HB
Tel: 01232 333315
A partnership of child loss support groups in Northern Ireland.